All Scripture references taken from the KJV of the HOLY Bible, unless otherwise indicated.

The Devil Loves Trauma by Dr. Marlene Miles

Freshwater Press, USA

ISBN: 978-1-960150-87-5

Paperback Version

Copyright 2023 by Dr. Marlene Miles

All rights reserved. No portion of this book may be copied, photocopied, emailed or held in any type of retrieval system without the express written approval of the Author.

Table of Contents

The Devil Loves Trauma 4
Shock 6
PTSD 9
Sudden Terror 12
Real or Rehearsed? 17
Holy Spirit, Come 21
Your Worst Life 24
Evil Human Agents 27
Evil Arrows 32
Doing What You've Always Done 34
Spirit Spouse: I HATE You 37
Flesh Reacts to Trauma 42
He Stole the Music 47
Be Free 51
God Is Binding Up Broken Hearts ... 63
You Are Powerful 68
What You See, What You Saw 70
PITCH BLACKNESS 79
The Trauma of Jesus 81
Let's Get Healed of Traumas 88
Other books by this author 94
Dear Reader 94

The Devil Loves Trauma

The Devil Loves Trauma

The devil loves trauma. He likes to inflict trauma, and often he uses the emotional kind--, broken hearts, against mankind, and womenkind. It's one of his signature moves.

I know this because God is binding up broken hearts. Why? Because there's so many broken hearts? Yes. Because of emotional trauma? Yes. Heart trauma? Yes.

Emotional stress is a favorite of the devil. There are many people in the Bible that went through traumas. I'll mention King David because the Book of Psalms is mostly about David's afflictions.

I'll mention in the New Testament Apostle Paul. He had a lot of traumatic experiences, too. He got beat up, sea tossed, locked in prison, and he had a thorn in the flesh.

There were many women in the Bible who had traumas; they were afflicted and abused. They were oppressed and there were many widows, which is essentially, single mothers. Sound familiar?

We might as well start out with Adam and Eve. They got evicted from paradise. That had to be traumatic.

So, trauma is a response to something that's deeply distressing or disturbing that happens to you. It is a disturbing event that surpasses the ability to cope.

Shock

Trauma can be physical, such as a car, sports, or a haphazard, freak, accident. Some traumas may be expected, as what people endure through war. There could be unexpected warlike situations, such as in a city. Or at a grocery store, mall, a movie theater? A sidewalk? A nightclub. A boardwalk. A church. Or a school--, an elementary school, or a college, for example.

Even when trauma is physical, it is *also* emotional.

Trauma is also emotional because the response to the terrible event, like the accident, or rape, or natural disaster invokes the soul of a person. The entire soul and spirit of a man is employed to try to handle this situation.

I remember once being enticed to sin, and it really was enticing. By use of my entire being, spiritually --, NO, it was sin, and totally wrong. When I engaged my soul on this matter, even though my spirit, led by the Holy Spirit was the first and final decision. The enticing sinner wanted to know why. For this reason my soul stood up for me and answered, *"I have no place to file this in my memory, and I know I won't forget it."*

Enticing as it was, it would have been a trauma to me.

The soul of a person is engaged after trauma to try to understand it, and put it away, file it away. If the trauma is not filed away, it will be thought upon, worried about every day and oppress the traumatized person.

Immediately after a trauma, sometimes there is shock to the system--, shock and denial. This is physiological. When trauma is physical it engages every system of the human body. When it is emotional it still engages the body systems even though no bones are broken.

Later on, there may be flashbacks, strained relationships, chronic situations and symptoms such as migraines, and other body symptoms. Shock is critical; it is brought on by a sudden drop in the blood flow in the body. It can result from trauma, heat stroke, blood loss, allergic reaction, severe infection, sepsis, poisoning, or severe burns.

PTSD

Sigmund Freud noticed that World War II veterans didn't just recall the violence that they had endured and experienced in the war, but they were actually **reliving** it, in the present. And that's when we first learned that experiences that people have can really shatter the psyche, they can shatter the mind, especially in cases of overwhelming violence. Post traumatic stress disorder does not know if something happened, or if it is *still* happening.

That event cannot be put away, filed away, if not forgotten, at least suppressed. Because of that it oppresses the person traumatized.

The devil loves this because he's got your mind open, as if you've opened a filing cabinet to look and look and look to see where a certain file goes. You never place the file anywhere, so the cabinet is just open.

Trauma OPENs a man up to demonic oppression and entrance.

Until that cabinet is closed, it is as though everything else stops while this file situation is dealt with. If it is never dealt with, or healed, the person is now suspended in that time and in that trauma. It is an anesthetic of sorts because now the devil can work somewhere else in your life, but you may not notice because you are focused on this PAIN, emotional, and/or physical.

Did this thing happen to a person, or is it *still* happening? If it's in the memory, in the soul, if it's in *your* memory, **it's real**. And, it will keep replaying, so it is currently happening again and again. Until Jesus heals it.

Until Jesus heals the person.

The devil loves this kind of trauma, he uses this kind of trauma. This kind of trauma doesn't just happen to soldiers and veterans. We are all prone to it as human beings. It is our natural human response, and it is not a fault in human; it is one of the things that makes us human. It is the devil who is exploiting our humanity whenever he can.

We all need Jesus.

Sudden Terror

Trauma can be a one-time thing, an acute trauma. It could be a chronic thing, such as domestic violence, or any kind of serial abuse. It happens in war and warlike situations that I've mentioned, such as terroristic events. Or trauma can be chronic, as for a soldier is in a real war.

Trauma occurs as a result of fires, earthquakes, tornadoes, hurricanes, floods, tsunamis, monsoons, any sudden, dangerous change in the environment, whether there is destruction or not.

Just the fear of a thing can be traumatic on its own. Do you know how many people seek shelter if they even *think* a thunderstorm is coming their way? I use

Wisdom in adverse weather situations. From childhood to now, I have seen and heard lightning strike three times with my own eyes, and once I saw it take down a standing object, similar to a tree.

Once I was stranded in my vehicle, having reached my home but not soon enough to get into the house before the downpour. I sat in my car waiting for the sudden storm to be over. Across the city street, with on street parking, just a few feet from where I sat in my car, I watched lighting bounce from one car, to a second, to a third, and saw the huge sparks grounded each time by the rubber tires on each of the vehicles.

My thought? *I'm in a car.* Then, of course, I was praying. Wouldn't you be?

Yeah, I don't play with weather, but with God we know He will protect us, so we balance healthy respect with Godly fear.

If someone raised their hand to hit you, but they did not hit you, that is still, legally an **assault**. If you *feel* threatened, that is an assault, legally speaking.

Job said the thing that he greatly feared had come upon him. ***Greatly fearing*** is a trauma. The devil can use that as well. We have not been given a *spirit of fear,* so if we are in fear, fearing, or ***greatly fearing*** then we are hosting a *spirit* that the Lord has not given us. We are hosting a demonic *spirit* that opens the door for other negative *spirits*.

If a person in the natural caused you to ***greatly fear,*** that is as an assault, whether it is a one-time assault, or if you ***greatly fear*** every day of your life because you live with or regularly see a person that you don't trust or are afraid of. Bullies are responsible for creating this in others; they cause their victims to fear, and *greatly fear* them.

Losing everything, as in destruction, losing everyone or losing even one someone is devastating. Even losing your pet is traumatic. I lost a goldfish once, and that was enough for me. But losing a person, someone special and not being able to cope with it brings on major trauma.

There is psychological and emotional trauma, and the mind is damaged after living through this, or anything else that is extremely frightening.

Some people like horror movies. They like to be afraid, as if trauma is entertainment. It is not, and I'm not a fan of that. I do not like my day, or my life traumatized in any way.

The thing that is in you will attract more of itself, like itself. Horror movies and the like open portals for the devil and his imps to get into you and your life.

> Do not be afraid of sudden terror. Nor trouble from the wicked when it comes. For the Lord will be your confidence and will keep your foot from being caught.

Proverbs 3:25 NKJV

Sudden terror is why I don't like horror movies. If the Bible tells us to not be afraid of it, why would I *seek* it out? Some people seek pain, or need pain to "feel alive." Deliverance is needed in that case. None of us should need horror, terror, or fear to make us feel *alive*.

Unresolved effects of trauma basically put a human in survival mode.

Real or Rehearsed?

Living and reliving traumas and sudden terrors keeps a person chronically in survival mode. Following, are some of the things that happen to a person as they go through trauma. After the trauma, unless healed and delivered, they are in survival mode, which are the exact same symptoms of still being IN the trauma. There may be intrusive thoughts about it, can't stop thinking about it. Out of the blue, here comes a thought, a flashback, nightmares, night terrors, visual flashbacks, loss of memory and concentration difficulties, confusion, mood swings, disorientation are all symptoms of survival mode.

Oh, but there are more, such as avoidance of things you used to like to do. Avoidance of doing things that trigger memories of the event. You won't go to *that* place. You won't go to *that* building. You don't even want to take *that* street if at all possible. If you lost your house to a fire or in any other way, you don't want to go to the land or the place where it was.

You might go into social isolation and withdrawal, and you might stop doing things you used to love to do. All of this is survival mode. These signs happen to be the same signs as witchcraft attack.

You might be jumpy, hyper, hypervigilant, expecting danger around every corner, super tired, heartbeat is racing, can't sleep, muscle spasms, sexual dysfunction, and changes in eating habits.

Vague complaints of aches in the body may start, but no one can find anything wrong with you. Fear, OCD, and detachment from other people rounds out the list of common human responses to unresolved trauma.

Or you might try to shut down your emotions altogether, so you don't *feel*. People describe this as going numb--. When they just can't handle a situation, or don't want to feel, because *feeling* it is too painful. This is especially true of emotional pain. Guilt, shame, self-pity, depression, anger, anxiety, and panic attacks can all be part of the picture, as well.

Trauma, survival mode, witchcraft attack, and add to that, soul captivity, all share the same symptoms, to varying degrees.

Your memory is trying to save your life, all the while keeping you *from* life. These responses or any combination of them prove that the person who has not gotten past a trauma has been captured by the devil. They are in captivity, and essentially on lockdown with no prison bars.

When the trauma occurred, your soul was exposed, and the devil got in, or sent in whatever evil *spirits* he chose to send. If you are not living life to the fullest, God's way, then at least part of your soul is captive.

Survival mode is captivity.

You can't live your best life in survival mode.

Whoa! We all need Jesus!

Holy Spirit, Come

I'm not trying to prove to anyone that witchcraft attacks are real. Evil arrows are real. As I've said before, you don't have to believe in witchcraft to be attacked by it. The person practicing the craft must believe in it. The perfect person to attack *is* the person who mocks it or doesn't believe that it is real.

Yet, even a person who sustains a witchcraft attack may look, to exhaustion, for the natural reasons as to why they are going *through*. Again, it's sudden. It can be subtle; it could happen in your sleep, and you could know nothing about an attack. Wake up the next morning, and it seems nothing happened, and when you go to the doctor, the doctor can find nothing wrong with you. But you start to feel all kinds of weird symptoms.

Witchcraft, unopposed is powerful and dangerous.

Believing that witchcraft exists, doesn't mean that you now practice it; it means that you are aware of it and hopefully protecting yourself against evil arrows. We can't see germs, but we protect ourselves from them in any number of ways.

For those who believe that they can protect themselves from witchcraft attack by not believing in it--, Baby, your mind is not that developed, or powerful. There is a whole lot of stuff in this world that I don't believe in, but it exists. I don't believe in unicorns, yet it is mentioned in the Bible. I cannot be so ignorant and prideful to believe that if <u>*I*</u> don't believe in it, then it is not. To not believe something is true when someone speaking from the Word of God is telling you that it is, smacks of pride, ignorance, and an *unteachable spirit.*

The converse is true, to believe that something *is* when it clearly is not. The emperor believed in his new clothes, yet he was naked, as was the Church of Laodicea in Revelation 3:17.

This problem is greater than most realize. It is the Holy Spirit that brings one into all Truth. Not being able to reach or attain to, get, or receive Truth is a sign that one does not have the Holy Spirit. Ask God for the Holy Spirit; ask God daily for fresh anointing and a new level of Grace to hear, receive, and understand Truth.

Your Worst Life

If you look at the symptoms, we just discussed, how will you function in your daily life with all that going on? People in survival mode often make very bad decisions, making the downward spiral, even more noticeable and much worse.

This is not what God intended for us.

Just like hell, which is custom made, evil arrows that are fired against you are also customized to bring you the most trauma. Why? Because the devil loves trauma. Because he can use that. These attacks open up a person's soul and the devil uses that opening to get into a person's life, into their business --, into that person.

A witchcraft attack traumatizes a person. This is problematic because how can you be traumatized by something that doesn't exist? How can you be traumatized by something invisible? Well, that was the goal, witchcraft is *occultic*, that means it is *hidden*. It is especially hidden to the person who doesn't believe that it exists, and it is designed to be hidden from the person who **is** aware that it exists.

Occultists hope they have a barrier to you seeing what they are doing, and if you are a naysayer, then you also put up your **own** barrier. It's like having blinds and curtains at a window that you really need to see through.

Many witches and occultic people are "friends" with the people they are shooting at. They smile in your face, but behind your back, at night, they may be in a coven with a dozen or so others casting spells and making incantations against individual enemies, or collective enemies, because they get together and work together against any name that is brought before the group. That is another reason why witchcraft is powerful, many times there is more than one of them against maybe just one person who is expecting nothing.

Biblical truth: one can put a thousand to flight, and two, ten thousand. The unsaved man who is not praying--, if he believes he is saved and is not, he is praying amiss, because who is he praying to? Saved man is praying and putting his 1000 to flight--, if he would get together with like-minded saints and pray, he would be at a higher level of being able to use angelic forces for his life and protection; he could put 10,000 to flight.

Witchcraft attack creates and mimics the human response to trauma. Trauma opens the door for the devil to enter into a person's life.

Evil Human Agents

Anyone who willfully traumatizes another person is working for the devil. If they're doing it on purpose, or not--, even if they're deceived. If they're a *blind witch*, they're still working for the devil.

What's an evil arrow? You may not think it's real. It is. *Arrows* represent a spell or curse, hex, vex, jinx, or an incantation. Anything. Evil arrows are shot from the kingdom of darkness to mankind. But it must come through people. The devil uses evil, ignorant, captured, or deceived people. It is illegal for any *spirit* to operate in the Earth without the permission of a human. It is for this same reason that we must agree with Heaven to make some things happen in the Earth. However, not agreeing with Heaven is the same as agreeing with Hell, because the devil is the prince of this world, and his way is default.

Unless you do something about it.

These arrows are shot because the devil hates you. The devil hates mankind. The devil is jealous of mankind. We get to be redeemed. He doesn't.

The devil is constantly trying to use or destroy mankind, it just depends on his purposes that day. So evil arrows from the kingdom of darkness come through the hands of your enemies. They could be people you know, or random wicked people. You could be the target of a coven where your household witch, fake friend, or unknown person has just decided or been instructed by the devil to shoot evil arrows at humans, especially Christians, and maybe you.

If you don't believe in anything else, you need to believe in God, and pray for protection. Other idols such as good luck charms, dream catchers, evil eye jewelry and the like, won't protect you. All that stuff is evil itself. Each has an evil idol attached to it. Satan cannot cast out Satan.

(Read my book, <u>This Is Not That, How to Keep Demons from Coming at You</u>.)

Without Jesus, your only protection against evil arrows is to be SIN FREE. No matter how much you think of yourself, no human is sin free. Only Jesus was sin free, the rest of us sin and fall short, pretty much daily. Every morning there are new mercies of God. Every day we need to pray for Mercy. Every day we not only need to forgive 70 X 7, but we also probably need to be *forgiven* 70 X 7 by Our Father, which art in Heaven who will forgive us our trespasses (sins) as we forgive others who trespass against us.

Arrows that come at you could be intended for you, and expertly aimed at you.

Or, you could just be collateral damage because you may be *near* somebody that an arrow is aimed at, or in the vicinity of the intended victim, if there is an attack in a public place, on public transport, or in a vehicle, for instance. This is why it is so dangerous to hang out with known enemies of God. They could be under judgment from God, or they could be easy victims of witchcraft attack if they are blatant sinners. The arrows will definitely hit a blatant sinner.

An "innocent" person could be collateral damage if the archer, the shootist can't even shoot straight. Like in the western movies of long ago--, *"They don't 'shoot good.'"* Don't be in the wrong place at the wrong time. We pray the Lord will direct your steps.

This is another reason for you to stay away from people that you know who are up to no good, pretty much on a daily basis. Even if you don't feel or you know that you're not in so much evil that an arrow should hit you. Because remember, the curses are not supposed to come unless there's a cause, unless there's some sin or evil in your life. By cause, we don't mean the witch's cause – because the witch wants to shoot the arrow, the cause is SIN, or iniquity in the intended victim.

Get your life organized. Get saved. Get filled with the Holy Sirit. Walk upright before the Lord, as much as possible. Stay prayed up. Live a fasted life and submit to the teachings and convictions of the Holy Spirit. In this is your protection.

Just stay away from the other people who are bad like that, and you know it.

Evil Arrows

Evil arrows are real. Just studying for this book, I've seen at least 77 different types of evil arrows. There may be as many as 100 or more. Different arrows are designed to bring different custom-made afflictions onto their *named* victims. Here's a few, in no special order, an arrow of affliction, an arrow of marital delay, arrow of miscarriage , an arrow of failure, and arrow of poverty, an arrow of the grave, an arrow of shame or reproach, an arrow of hatred, an arrow of infirmity, an arrow of demotion, an arrow of disaster.

Do I need to go on? I didn't think so.

I'd like to also take the time to let people who have not accepted Jesus as your Lord and Savior, or those who have backslidden and plan to stay backslidden, know that Hell is real. The devil is real, and he has wicked plans for you right here on Earth, and even *wickeder*.

The Most Wicked (the devil) plans for you to be in Hell for eternity. And for people who think that after this life you just die and take a dirt nap, that that's all there is, better know this: your spirit, the spirit is eternal. There's gonna be a customized hell just for you, if that's where you end up. Please don't! There are customized damnation, customized torments just for you, after this life in the afterlife.

Doing What You've Always Done

Death? There will not be just nothing. It will not just be a quiet dirt nap. There is no after-party, people. You're gonna be put to work. You don't work for the devil, you may say in protest.

What you are doing here on Earth, whatever you're good at now, whatever you're trying to do now, that's kind of a clue. That's an inkling. It's a picture of what you're going to be doing for the devil, if you land in hell.

So the evil that we see in movies and on TV, the evil scientists, the diabolical people doing diabolical things, you better get ready to work, because that's probably what you'll have to do for the devil 24/7.

There is no rest for the wicked. Isaiah 48:22. There is no peace, says the Lord for the wicked.

Your eternal hell assignment *may* be to traumatize humans. I know a man who is obsessed with sex. He, out of his own mouth stated that he would like to be like a rooster in a hen house and just do that all day long. This man believes he's saved, but the *spirit* that spoke that, through him---, the *spirit* that lives in him wants to fulfill *lust*.

If he, that man's real **human spirit** doesn't object and get delivered of that *spirit, it will have it's way by the man having what the man is saying.* In this way, the man is agreeing with Hell via the *spirit* that is in him, that is having all the "fun." In Eternity, that *spirit* is not getting into Heaven. So where will this "saved" man's soul go after death?

There is no afterparty, People.

Folks can be harassed by the devil, oppressed by the devil, or possessed by the devil. Those possessed, owned, and captive do what the devil wants them to do; they have no choice. They can fight it here on Earth, but after Earth, there is nothing they can do, but suffer, eternally.

Spirit Spouse: I HATE You

Of course, I will mention *spirit spouse* in this book. It seems that the sex-obsessed man is applying for the job of spirit spouse. I cannot say more right now. *I can't* because I hate spirit spouse with *perfect hate.*

Spirit spouse's job is serial defilement, among other things. Defilement is trauma. The man who desires and is involved in stud service in the Earth, while he is at least physically living this life, is auditioning for the job of *spirit spouse*. Of course, they have evil fallen angels for that, but this human male may already be a *physical spirit spouse* to any number of women, or men.

Spirit spouse, in the spirit, is gender fluid; it changes into whatever it needs to in order to attack it's victims.

Stud service men really think they are so desirable, but they do not realize the **TRAUMA** they inflict on women, and eventually the children they have. They are working like the devil, for the devil. The reward is usually only sex, and that by deception.

Pray God that whatever you are doing, whatever you think is fun, your living is not TRAUMATIZING the people you know and encounter, else, you are on remote for the devil without even realizing it.

Victims of such, cut your losses. Get out of those situationships and so-called relationships. Repent to God; break soul ties, move on with your life.

Yeah, there are some people who love to keep some mess going in families, at offices, and on their jobs. By so doing and stressing others, these emotionally and spiritually "messy" people inflict trauma on others and make them more susceptible to devil attack, or sending them into full blown survival mode. These busy bodies, gossipers, slanderers, and liars are channels of trauma; they are also working for the devil.

Think about that because the devil loves trauma, and if he can traumatize people, he can get into their lives, mess them up, steal from them, or kill him if he gets the opportunity.

The devil gets the "right" to do anything to mankind by accusing 24/7 at the Throne of God. He tries to win judgements against mankind. These evil judgments are so the devil can steal, kill, and destroy from the intended victim – on the lines of Job.

In the afterlife, how do you think that the devil's gonna make you work for him? Well, I don't know. Take a guess. Maybe he'll invoke fear in you, or lie to you, or torture you, or traumatize you until you come under his submission. This could be why the living keep praying, rest in peace over their dearly departed, because there's no peace, says the Lord, for the wicked. So don't die in sin, accept Jesus as your Lord and Savior now. Don't die unsaved. Don't die wicked, because there's no redemption after death. There's no rest for the wicked. You will not be able to say after death, *Oh, I didn't know, or I changed my mind.*

I'm telling you now, there is no redemption after death.

If you just want to be a smart Alec, why don't you go ahead and accept Jesus anyway, just in case I'm telling the truth, because I am. Can't hurt you to hedge your bets, *right*? Why don't you accept Jesus? Do it now.

The Bible gives us a picture of what the saved will be doing and what they'll be inheriting in the afterlife with God. But the afterlife with the devil--, where's that image? Where's that picture? Oh, it burned up in the house fire. You think you're tired now? No. There's no rest for the wicked--, 24/7. You will be perpetually working for the devil if you do not accept Jesus while you are living **this** life.

All the mockers are saying, *I'll take my chances.* **There are no chances after this one. This life--, this is the chance.** While there's life, there's hope. Accept Jesus as Savior and make Him the Lord of your life now.

Flesh Reacts to Trauma

Back to this trauma. Through trauma, if we're not prayed up, if we're not careful, if we are, or are not even *trying* to live a godly lifestyle, the devil is standing by, he's standing right there, to get into your life by offering you temptations that will corrupt you, pollute your body and give you over into sin. The only defense against it is being saved by Jesus Christ and observing the laws, and practicing the faith.

The first temptation after being traumatized is unforgiveness. The devil tempts you not to forgive the offender, giving you all the reasons why you can't forgive the offender. Depending on what *spirits* are in you, he may be successful at this level. Depending on what's in you, and your level of captivity, you may be powerless against the devil, and he may have his way in *your* life.

Then, there's the temptation of revenge. A form of revenge is pride, where **You'll show them**. You'll get a new *whatever* and make them jealous or wish they had stayed your friend. Can you see how all this is devil work, and not of the Spirit of God, at all?

So many things can open up doors for the devil to come in, Number 1 is our own sin. Number 2, as we just discussed, is **more sin**, but it approaches in a more subtle way: unforgiveness, resentment, bitterness. Unforgiveness brings on torment, and torment is from the devil.

These things are more grievous and give the devil permission, an invitation to live in your life, to live in your house--, your body even.

Involvement in the occult is very serious; it is not fun and games. It's real.

Sadly, many times, people come under demonic oppression due to abuse, it may be in their bloodline, but it is not their fault at all. But they may come under demonic harassment and oppression can be brought on by abuse of any kind. Having trauma forced on you still opens evil doors and can leave a person stunned, astonished, shocked--, defenseless.

Our normal human response to trauma is documented and known. The devil knows what that response is going to be, that's why we have to be smarter and know ourselves as well as what the human response to trauma is. We have to, by the power of Jesus Christ, know how to and be able to NOT have the anticipated or standard human response to assaults. **We need a God response to trauma to keep the devil out of our lives.**

Survival mode: we get to decide if we're gonna stay in it or not, if we're gonna do what the Lord says to do to come out of it. But when that trauma hits, the devil runs to it. Most of the time, he both created and **caused** the trauma, directly, or indirectly to open the door to your soul. That is what the devil uses to get into your life. He creates the trauma to allow the door to open.

It's kind of like in the movies some guys are trying to break into the bank, so they tape explosives to the vault door to blow it up so they can get in. It's the same thing. The devil creates a trauma in a life to blow it up, so he can get in. He doesn't mind trauma after trauma; he did that to Job.

Lord, help us all.

So, trauma is stored in our in our memories, in our minds, it's also stored in our bodies.

When the similar stress or the same stress comes back to you, will you have the same response? Or will you have God on board this time?

Humans have muscle memory; whatever we did last time, whatever we normally do, with the same stimuli, we do the same thing, again. If it was of God, then good. If it was not, then you may have just walked into another devil trap. Sad, when it's the same trap you walked into on your last birthday, or whenever he last did this evil thing to you.

He Stole the Music

There you are dancing, forming or renewing a dance covenant with that song, because you like that song. It might be a good song for you. It holds memories of a certain time in your life.

That's a good stress. Stress can be a trauma that the soul has to deal with; even a good stress is still stress.

Just because it's a good song, with a good beat or it reminds you of back in the day, doesn't mean that you should still be listening to it, or dancing to it. Listen to the words, seriously listen. I've been tuned in to words of songs more and more lately. I felt those songs were okay because there were no cuss words in them.

I was incorrect.

Years ago, a spiritual friend said, *"All love songs were misplaced songs to God, but men have sung them to women, and women to men."*

He was also incorrect.

Every secular song that is about something illicit is not a love song to God. Every secular song that is about people interacting in unholy alliances, especially under the cover of night is not misplaced adoration to God. These songs are from the evil marine kingdom, and they cause the artist AND the singer (you) to rehearse over and again giving *spirit spouse*, poverty and all other evil *spirits* entrance into your life. Into your night. Into your bed. You've made a covenant with those words of that song that you've spoken (sung) out of your own mouth making them <u>your</u> words.

The problems begin.

Now, you have to figure out what you've done and also how to get out of it.

Verbal covenant. Dance covenant – just tapping your foot, nodding your head, or outright dancing, you agree with the words of this song.

How many of us listen to the same song over and over again once we decide that it's our jam, or we just like it? We like the way the singer sings, and we want to hit those notes, so we practice it in and out of the shower? Forming covenants 24/7 whether we know it or not.

A song could be saying something *waaaaay* different than you think it is. I've been noticing not just songs from the marine kingdom, but once I listened to several songs by certain artists, I can now pinpoint which ones are working for the marine kingdom, whether *they* realize it or not.

In this way, we've invited evil *spirits* into our world, or at least trauma to open doors for the devil.

Going to concerts can be even worse than listening at home or in your personal time. At the concert is the mob mentality, and the channeling by the secular artist. Haven't you noticed from news reports how the same thing happens at every concert by a certain artist? And then, another something happens at another artist's concert? It all depends on what they are channeling, and therefore, what's in the atmosphere at their concerts.

When war broke out in Heaven and the devil was kicked out, he fell to Earth. The devil was the worship leader; he was music. He stole the music, so why wouldn't he be doing something with it?

Praise and worship music is a weapon in our own spiritual warfare.

Can't music also be used to the negative, as a weapon?

Be Free

There are good stressors and there are bad stressors. Trauma is a bad stress, and it's stored in your body, so your muscle memory, body memory just makes you do the same thing again. We're gonna pray in the Name of Jesus. We will ask the Lord to break that off of us today, in Jesus' Name.

So, because these memories and these traumas are stored in your mind and your body, that's the biggest part of the struggle. Our body and mind want to do what we've always done, but all of us should have our spirit man grown up, built up so much that the spirit man is directing what's going on and once the spirit man is directing things, this keeps the devil out of our lives, so we don't go into more of a downward spiral.

You have a powerful mind.

The Spirit of the Lord is upon me. In this passage below, we see the connection between the healing of a person's mind. There's soul which the mind is part of, needs deliverance from the bondage of trauma.

> The Spirit of the Lord GOD *is* upon Me,
> Because the LORD has anointed Me
> To preach good tidings to the poor;
> He has sent Me to heal the brokenhearted,
> To proclaim liberty to the captives,
> And the opening of the prison to *those who are* bound;
>
> Isaiah 61:1

What prison am I talking about here? Is the devil clever enough to have a person imprisoned in their own mind?

Yes.

Your body is not in jail. You get up every morning and you take the car or metro, or *whatever*, to work. You're free to move about the country, in or out of a face mask. You are free, but does your mind keep you from doing things that you should do, or things that you want to do?

If so, your mind is in prison, is it your mind or your soul, that is running your life? Or is your spirit man running your life? Let me know.

But a bird that stalks down his narrow cage can seldom see through his bars of rage.

His wings are clipped and his feet are tied, so he opens his throat to sing.

The caged bird sings with a fearful trill. Of things unknown, but longed for still. And his tune is heard in the distant hill, for the caged bird Sings of freedom.

Maya Angelou, *I Know Why the Caged Bird Sings*

Aren't there things in your life that you need to do, or want to do? There are things you know about, things you've seen, read about, and you want to do them, but you've not taken the steps to do it. That's not freedom. That's a bondage. That is your mind holding you captive because of the trauma, because of the things you've been through.

> About midnight, Paul and Silas were praying and singing hymns to God. And the other prisoners were listening to them, and suddenly a strong earthquake shook the foundations of the prison. And at once, the doors flew open and everyone's chains came loose.
>
> Acts 16:25-26,

There is freedom from this prison of the mind. There's freedom from traumas. There's freedom from hurts, losses, and grief. Paul and Silas were locked in a prison; instead of lamenting and woe-is-me-*ing*, which is the normal body, and mind response to being on lockdown, instead, Paul and Silas were praising and worshipping God. This is how you do not let the devil traumatize you or use the trauma that he himself may have inflicted on you. Even or if it was unexpected trauma against you, this is not how you let him use trauma against you, by staying in that place.

Being on lockdown is heartbreaking. So many things in this life can be heartbreaking for all of us, but thank God that God is binding up broken hearts.

We have to choose to have a whole different response than what the body thinks we're gonna do. Do not let your body run you. Do not let your mind, soul, and will run things. You have to let your spirit man, which is directed by the Spirit of God run your life. This is how you gain that freedom, so you're not in a cage.

In this way even when something traumatic has happened to you, you don't think on the people that are attached to those hurts. Don't think on the people that are attached to those disappointments, to those losses and sorrows. Don't spend your time on that because it will not prosper your mind or your soul. As a matter of fact, it will cause more imprisonment.

So don't dwell and think on the people that are attached to the hurts, the disappointments, the losses, the sorrows, the sadness, because thinking on them magnifies them. Thinking about it all day long or intermittently through the day magnifies them. And this is what you could end up doing if you keep your mind stayed on that instead of on God. You could blindly curse the people that are involved without even intending or realizing that you're doing it.

And then by doing this, *you* become the person shooting evil arrows. You become a *blind witch,* not even realizing you're doing it.

Continually thinking on them makes them into an idol and you could blindly idolize them. And this is gonna happen if you're thinking about them all day. God said to have no idols before Him. So obsessing on a person, be it positive or negative can idolize them. Don't do that.

Continuously thinking on them and these problems, you magnify the wrongs done to you, and you stay in unforgiveness and bitterness. These are all sins. And you stay in the flesh. There's no blessing in the flesh. Instead, we must walk by the Spirit, let the Holy Spirit direct our spirit man, so we don't fulfill the lust and the desires of the flesh.

By thinking on these things, we could conjure up things that we want or think we want. Some people call that manifesting. Except by the Holy Spirit, there's a thin line between manifesting something good and conjuring up something evil.

Still, when you continue to think on this evil, hurt, loss, and trauma, you'll end up hurting yourself more as you rehearse the wrongs done. Your body doesn't even know **when** this thing happened to you, or even if it happened already. So worrying about something that hasn't even happened confuses your mind and your body. And your body doesn't know if that thing is currently happening or not.

And by worrying--, you are really experiencing the negative event in the worst way because of your powerful mind. You're experiencing it at least once before you actually go through it, and you're experiencing it the in the worst way if your imagination just takes everything to the worst place. Then when it **really** happens, there you are experiencing it again. So, you're experiencing it more than once, depending on how often and how you worry, leading up to this actual event. But then after the event is over and you keep dwelling on it in your mind and your body, remember you've got body memory, therefore you may still think it's still happening to you, or that this evil happens every day.

You may wake up in the morning thinking, *Oh my goodness, I gotta go through that again.* Well. If you're gonna put your mind on it. And that memory, are you going to practice the memory, the body memory of it? Yeah, you're going to go through it again. A cascade of survival mode restarts for the day, and it's a serious downward spiral.

Instead of celebrating the new mercies of God this morning, you start your day out in dread.

This, unfortunately, is what people with PTSD are experiencing. It's gonna take the power and the Love of Jesus Christ to heal Post Traumatic Stress Disorder. The trauma and terror blow the vault door wide open where your spirit man and your soul should be safe inside.

Then there's the devil trying to come in.

This may sound trivial to you, but it wasn't for me. I had PTSD from the way my husband used to drive. It was torment. It was dangerous, and scary as all get out, but I didn't realize it at the time. **After** I stopped riding with him in the car, I realized what was wrong with me. It was his driving.

I'm not exaggerating. On the drive back from picking up a new vehicle, several states away, we were jolted from left to right for miles and miles of interstate. The next-to-new creampuff of a car beeped and sounded for 100's of miles. It felt like we were veered and jerked from left to right the whole trip. This was supposed to be a relaxing trip for us. Hubby complained about this car's steering mechanism all the way. Another state back I asked him if we shouldn't take the car back, like now.

Well, folks, the car had lane assist, and he was constantly out of the lane we should be in, and the car was trying to put him back in the right lane, and he fought it all the way. Hence, the veering, swerving, jolting and beeping. Yeah, you'd have PTSD from that, too.

I know another woman who will not ride with her fiancé anywhere. She meets him everywhere they go because of his exceptionally poor driving.

Trauma is trauma.

Keeping your mind on the trauma or the hurts, the disappointment, the sadness, causes you to continue to traumatize yourself. This may be the crux of this book; but there may be more that God wants to share with us.

If you keep thinking about it, you continue to traumatize yourself. So an evil arrow hit you. The downward spiral started, and now if you keep your mind stayed on it and you have a body response to it, you're continuing to do the extra work yourself. The devil introduces a trauma to you, and then you destroy yourself by keeping your mind on it. The Blood of Jesus is against this. Don't traumatize *yourself*. The devil loves trauma--, physical trauma, emotional or mental trauma; he uses all kinds of upset.

The predictable human response to trauma makes people predictable --, controllable. It makes them malleable, manipulatable. Don't traumatize yourself by dwelling in the place of hurt and evil. Don't stay in that emotional trauma and grief because the devil is using it. Continuously dwelling on hurts and wrongs and disappointments and what people did to you, and even planning revenge keeps you in the past. It keeps that door open for the devil, while you relive it over and over again with all that pain and sorrow.

Shut the front door! Shut all the doors to your soul.

God Is Binding Up Broken Hearts

But God is binding up broken hearts.

> The Spirit of the Lord God is upon me because the Lord hath anointed me to preach good tidings unto the meek. he sent me to bind up the broken hearted, to proclaim liberty to the captives, and the opening of the prison to them that are bound. Isaiah 61:1.

Where the devil likes to cause and inflict emotional trauma against man, God is binding up broken hearts.

Trust this, you want God to bind up your broken heart. If God is touching your heart, you are still able to feel God's presence, you can still hear Him, it is the best indication that your heart is not stolen and captive by the devil. Take the comfort that God is giving you through His Spirit. **Let Him** bind your broken heart.

Why is God binding up broken hearts? To keep them from bleeding? yes. To keep them from crying? Yes. From leaking? Yes. To keep them from getting worse? Yes. And to keep infection out? Yes. To keep the devil out. The Devil is an infection? Yes. Certainly yes.

So, until these broken hearts heal, God binds them up, because the devil runs to the broken heart, a traumatized heart. And just as a hurricane, or tornado can break a window, you quickly put up plyboard and nail it up, to keep whatever out that's not supposed to go in through that door, that window. God is binding up the broken heart to keep the devil out of it. Thank You, Lord.

God binds it up. because the heart is the source, the fountain that pumps the blood, and the life is in the blood, It pumps the blood and life to the rest of the human body.

If the devil could infiltrate and poison the heart, the body's central system, that poison could quickly get to the rest of the body. Easy. Peasy.

So don't traumatize *yourself*. Don't stay in the doldrums or in the past with all its hurts. If you need support and help, look for it, reach out to your pastor or counselor, intercessors, or ministers of deliverance to pull yourself out of it.

It's very dangerous to have a broken heart. Allowing yourself to be soul tied to another also afflicts the heart, affects the heart, and weakens it. Don't stay blue and keep talking about it and singing the Blues about it and staying soul tied and traumatized.

If you can't get out of it on your own, call someone, call a friend. Pray, of course. Call someone. Because God is binding up broken hearts until they're healed--, until God can heal it.

Still, you have a part in the healing of your own heart. And you've got to agree with God so He can do His work in you.

Because a caged bird would sing stands on the grave of dreams. His shadow shouts on a nightmare scream. His wings are clipped and his feet are tied, so he opens his throat to sing.

Maya Angelou, *I Know Why the Caged Bird Sings*

Jesus, Himself was touched with the feelings of our infirmities. We're not saying don't feel--, go through your feelings, yes. But don't get used to all the attention and sympathy. Learn how to receive the comfort of people. Sympathy moves people to compassion and into action to help you. Sympathy is a powerful motivator, and it can provoke a lot of ministry. But God gave people 30 days in the wilderness to get over the loss of Moses. And God says that saved people don't grieve as others because we have a hope. We're going to see our loved ones again.

Don't let the devil trick you into staying in grief because you like the attention and *stuff* that it gets you. That's a trick of the devil because it props open another door for the devil to mosey on through.

Read the book: **Seasons of Grief**, by this author.)

You Are Powerful

God binds up broken hearts because of your powerful mouth. You've got a powerful mind, you've got a powerful heart, you have a powerful mouth.

God allowed Adam to **<u>name</u>** everything, and whatsoever Adam called it, that was its name, (Genesis 2:19). With your powerful mouth, God allows you to **name** things as well. You call a thing blessed; it's blessed. You call a thing cursed, unless you're trying to reverse what God has said, that will come to pass. The wise man knows that what God has blessed, he can't curse it. If God has cursed it, it's cursed.

It's like on your computer if you're the administrator of your office software program. You could write a note, or a report, but no one can change it, only you. My software at work is like that. No one can overwrite what I wrote. I can change it, I can correct it, I can delete. No one can change what I've put in place. I'm not God, and neither are you, so do not try to overwrite what He has established already; be careful with your powerful mouth.

Call a thing successful, it's successful. You call a thing a miserable failure, and it will become that. Do not speak curses over your own life or over the lives of people you know and see.

What You See, What You Saw

This is why you need faith, because without faith it's impossible to please God. God calls us blessed. Are we--, right now in the natural are we blessed? God, by faith is speaking over us. God speaks a lot of things over us by faith; He calls things that are not as though they were. That is, God is **naming** us Hallelujah.

Whatever God has named us, that's what we are and that's what we *become* unless we willfully disobey and rebel against Him.

The same is true for you if you're in the Kingdom of God. But if you are without faith and you've gone through trauma, all you will do is repeat what you see, what you saw. What you see--, what you saw. So, if you've been through this trauma and you've experienced devastating events, your mind may want to just repeat over and over again what it sees, what it saw. And maybe it's just your mind's way of trying to reconcile and settle what happened. The file cabinet is wide open and you're trying to find a place to put this file, this event, this memory. Does it fit this way, or maybe if I turn it--, it will fit that way.

If God has not cursed it, you can't either, unless a person enters into a curse on his own. Sin enrolls us in curses, the Curse of the Law. We are the administrator of our Earth lives by having and using our own free will.

Maybe it's your mind's way of trying to get sympathy and stuff, repeating it and repeating. Like scenery in an old cartoon, it just keeps repeating over and over.

God is binding up broken hearts, because out of the abundance of your heart, your powerful mouth will speak. And what do you say? You say what you see in the natural if you're a natural man, if you're a flesh man.

If you have faith, you say what God says.

If you're a natural man in the flesh, you say what you see and you say what you saw. That is all you do. You say what *your* expectation is. That is without faith.

But with faith, you will say what God says about you in the Word of God, what God said about you in your ear, what the prophet prophesied over you, what you heard in the Spirit after you prayed.

Because the flesh man likes to just be a know-it-all he's saying. I know what happened. I was there. I saw it. This is what happened. Oh, I've seen this before. This is what's gonna happen. But if you're still in shock and disbelief. You might just rehearse this thing over and over in your mind, because you're trying to find a file in your mind to file it away.

But God.

With faith, God says, **Behold, I'm gonna do a new thing.** Even if you've been through hurt, trauma, loss, and grief, God says He'll do a new thing for you.

Faith comes by hearing, so you need to listen to God. So, both seeing and hearing are important to get out of the past. Because of what happened in the past, without faith, we only have expectancy. And you're expecting the same results even though God says He is going to do a new thing.

God is binding the broken hearts. He's guarding your broken heart. And especially if it's broken and busted and traumatized. Because out of your mouth flow the issues of life, and out of the abundance of the heart, the mouth will speak. God is binding up that broken heart to keep you from speaking evil things over your life. He is keeping you from speaking traumatized things over your life. And over any part of your life, with your broken heart.

In that state, if you narrate and prophesy, what you will or won't do, what you want to happen, what you don't want to happen, if you're a natural or a carnal man, you're probably saying the opposite of what God says about you.

Remember, some things just can't happen in Earth until you agree with God. Most often a broken heart will agree with the devil instead of with Our Father.

Angels are on the ready, waiting for your words, to cause what you say to come to manifestation for you. If you're disagreeing with God by speaking with that broken heart--, Lord have Mercy!

Either nothing will happen. Or God will just impose His will and something miraculously good will happen anyway, whether we deserve it or not. Maybe God will just give in and give you the broken hearted prophecy that you for some reason want to endure, thereby creating evil timelines for your life. Cursing your own life? Don't do it.

God is binding up broken hearts. And He's binding up your broken heart to keep your broken heart from speaking over the lives of others as well.

> They sharpen their tongues like swords and aim cruel words like deadly arrows.
> (Psalm 64:3 NIV)

Do not be an evil arrow shooter. There are a lot of broken-hearted, divorced, or widowed parents who speak over their children. They think they are speaking edifying or comforting words to them, but they're really diminishing, limiting, harmful words.

Words like, *Oh, don't trust this one, don't trust that, don't do that. No, I did that and look what happened to me.*

You want to minister to your children from a place of wholeness and peace. You want to minister to your own life and over your friends from place of wholeness and peace. Not from a place of hurt.

Review the Book of Job to and note all the negative things that came out of his wife's mouth, his friends' mouths, and even his own mouth.

God is guarding and binding your heart to keep the devil out of it. And to keep evil out of it because out of the abundance of the heart, the mouth will speak. When the heart is bound up, that broken heart cannot suggest things for your powerful mouth to say.

And binding up that heart, swaddling that heart, God is wrapping His Love around it. He encases the heart and therefore the mouth to restrain the mouth from saying ungodly things. The risk is that spoken things may come to pass if your guardian demon, is there, because they will try to make that evil that you spoke, happen to you.

I have said many stupid things in my youth that I never should have said. Too bad for me, I've gotten a lot of those stupid things that I said. I'm the one who created evil timelines for myself. That was not smart. Take the lesson and don't repeat my mistakes.

OK, I've repented and renounced those ignorant words, and I have forgiven myself. You must learn to quickly repent and move on. Forgive yourself and move on, in Jesus' Name.

The *infection*, that is, the devil, cannot get into a broken heart that is bound by the Lord. Because when God shuts up something, it's shut. Nobody can get in it. When He opens doors, nobody can close them again.

Where a wound is dressed and cleaned, that is, there's been repentance, renunciation, and the gauze and Love of the Holy Spirit is wrapped around this wound, you're on your way to healing.

If not, this thing could remain broken. It could fester; it could get worse, or a spiritual sepsis could set in. Sepsis leads to spiritual death. Spiritual death is being cut off completely from the life of God. That is what Jesus was lamenting when He was having to go to the Cross, losing all connection with God. That is not something you want.

Ever.

PITCH BLACKNESS

When your electricity goes out in a storm or for some other reason, you may find yourself in a pitch black room. There is not even the light of a clock, the cable box, your cell phone--, there is no light.

Pitch Blackness, and you're struck by the stone cold silence.

There's no ambient street light streaming through your room window. No moonlight. Nothing.

You have no idea of which way to go or if you should move in any direction at all. You are just frozen in pitch blackness. Now imagine that same pitch blackness with screams of torment--, and some of those screams are yours. That's hell. You need to run to Jesus and salvation while you can. Because hell is real.

Renounce sin, repent, and turn from sin, and to Jesus.

Believe in your heart that Jesus is the Son of God, and that He came to Earth, died for our sins, and on the third day God raised him from the dead. Say it with your powerful mouth. And that is how you receive salvation. Make Jesus the Lord of your life.

> If you declare with your mouth, "Jesus is Lord," and believe in your heart that God raised him from the dead, you will be saved. For it is with your heart that you believe and are justified, and it is with your mouth that you profess your faith and are saved, (Romans 10:9-10)

Receive deliverance, be healed from all your traumas, receive the Holy Spirit, resist the devil and live a godly lifestyle.

The Trauma of Jesus

The devil pulled out all the stops when he tried to traumatize Jesus into submission. He tried from Jesus' arrival on Earth.

If Jesus had chosen the human response to any of the traumas that He went through, where would we all be now?

Lost.

Born in a barn, placed in the animals' feeding trough for a bed. No wonder He said the Son of Man has no where to lay His head. Even if He had a *where*, what would have been His time to just sleep and do little to nothing. Jesus was on the run from Herod at a very early age. He was pursued constantly by the Pharisees and Sadducees, yet it was His habit from youth to go to the Temple daily. We let reasons tinier than that keep us from going to church.

Yet, they sought to find some law to permit them to capture and do away with Him.

Are these not stresses?

His idea of a break from daily life was a 40 day fast in the Wilderness. Do you think He was in the Wilderness to sleep?

On the boat on the way to the Gadarenes, Jesus slept. Jesus was going to do ministry; His disciples? They were probably just on the boat for the ride. Jesus' human body needed rest, as do all of ours. In Jesus-speak, to sleep meant death. We are supposed to work while it is yet day--, so when was Jesus just *sleeping*?

In Gethsemane, Jesus asked the Disciples can you watch and pray for one hour? One hour was a small ask, since a prayer watch is 3 hours, not one. We know that Jesus didn't just spend a few minutes in prayer--, He was *all in,* probably constantly talking to and hearing from God. If that were not the case, being cut off on that Cross would not have been a traumatic thought, or a traumatic experience for Him.

Jesus, being all God means He was all Spirit. At night when men sleep the spiritual world does not. Do you think Jesus was caught unawares at night? Of course, He wasn't. Jesus was doing something in other realms and dimensions all the time. How can I say that?

John the Baptist baptized Jesus around age 30, in three years' time, Jesus' work was done. We know it was done because Jesus gave up the Ghost; no one took His life; He laid it down. Jesus also said, "**It is finished**."

Jesus wasn't cut off, cut short, or caught flatfooted. He did everything He was sent here to do. Now, we know the Grace and Spirit and Power of God was on Him and with Him, but to successfully complete the most impactful ministry in the history of all ministries in three years meant that Jesus was not snoozing, napping, lazing around and chilling. He did the will of the one who sent Him.

Some folks take 50+ years to do their ministry, to do their life's work. Those folks are human, like you and I. Humans take longer, because sometimes we sleep. We nap. We take vacations.

The devil thought the trauma was the ridicule, the beatings, the pain, the torture, the blood, the humiliation, and the death. To a plain, regular human, that would have been the anticipated response or reaction.

Jesus had another whole response that the devil, and all of mankind had never seen before. When you're playing chess, you want to turn your pawns into Kings (and Queens), but when you already start out as the King, as Jesus did, there are no pawns that the devil can employ to take you down.

The devil couldn't figure out what trauma to send Jesus to get Him into the flesh. In the flesh is the devil's realm, where he can defeat humans easily. But there was no Law that could take Jesus out. Jesus walked in the Spirit and there is NO LAW against the Fruit of the Spirit.

Jesus was all God and all Spirit so His response to anything, any trauma would be the way God responds, not the way flesh reacts.

If Jesus had gone into survival mode, He would certainly have survived, but none of us would have. For this, we should take the lesson and be eternally grateful that insult after insult, assault after assault, trauma after trauma, Jesus chose us instead of Himself.

He who loses his life gains it, (Matt 16:25). Jesus modeled that to perfection.

Jesus said, that **the** prince of this world had (has) nothing in Him. That means that Jesus could not be accused by the devil. He could not be judged by the devil, or his evil human agents. Jesus could not be killed or put to death. Jesus could not be defiled or cut off from God. Jesus lacked nothing for this life, and Jesus was not sick. Ever.

Jesus' choice, and by God's plan was to lay down His life in substitution for us.

None of us are perfect, but the fewer *idols* we serve, the fewer demonic *spirits* we host, the more effective we can be in life and in our ministry. The fewer problems we will have in this life, the fewer evil arrows that will hit us, the more successful we will be, and the easier it will be to invoke the power of forgiveness, just as Jesus did.

Forgive them, for they know not what they do.

Forgiveness is the file where you store hurts, disappointments, losses, willful traumas from known assailants, rather than holding on and rehearsing them to your own downward cascade of events in life. Forgiveness is the file in that cabinet that you are looking for after a trauma. Don't just stand there with your soul open to be attacked by the devil, like a kid standing in the refrigerator who can't see the orange juice that's right in front of him, in the same place where it always is.

Forgiveness is in the same place where it always is; you don't need to even look for it that hard.

That does not mean that you don't pray against the wicked powers behind evil things that happen to you, but we don't hold on to unforgiveness, or attack known or suspected flesh and blood.

Let's Get Healed of Traumas

Father in the Name of Jesus Christ, and by the power of His Cross and His Blood, we bind up the power of any evil *spirit*, and command them not to block our prayers.

We bind the power of Earth, air, water, fire, the netherworld, and the satanic forces of nature. We break any curses, hexes, or spells sent against us and declare them null and void.

We break the assignments of any *spirits* sent against us and send them to Jesus to deal with them, as He will.

We ask You to bless our enemies by sending your Holy Spirit to lead those who will repent, to repentance and conversion.

Lord, I bind all interaction and communication of evil human spirits as it pertains to me.

I ask for the protection of the shed Blood of Jesus Christ as I pray this prayer.

Thank You, Lord, for divine protection. Send Your warrior angels to give me the win in this battle.

In the Name of Jesus Christ, I command you devil, not to interfere with this prayer. I cut you off by the Sword of the Spirit from the stirring up of grief, fear, fear of any kind, emotional, or any other kind of trauma induced problems, and I command quiet, in the Name of Jesus.

Lord, in the Name of Jesus, I forgive everyone who has offended, hurt, harmed, embarrassed, or traumatized me in any way.

Lord, go back to the moment in time of this trauma, to that broken relationship, that broken heart, the disappointment, the loss, the sadness that continues to influence me, Lord. Jesus, take the sting, the bite, the hurt, the pain, the trauma, the loss out of that event so it no longer harms me.

Lord, transform that day, that hour, that moment, that event in my mind and let me see that if You allowed it, You used it to bless me or teach me and enlarge me. Lord, let me see You there. In that moment, in that time, ministering to me right at that time.

I know You were there. You would never leave me or forsake me.

Lord, forgive me for my part in allowing that evil to come upon my life.

And I know that what the devil meant for evil, what he meant for my harm, that You can turn it for my good.

Spirit of Trauma, exit my life now, exit my life forever. The angels of God escort you out now and take you to the place assigned to you. It is not with me. Not any longer.

Spirit of grief, Exit my life now. Exit my life forever. The angels of God escort you out now and take you to the place assigned for you. It is not with me. Not any longer.

Spirit of loss, sadness, disappointment, sympathy, exit my life now. Exit my life forever. The angels of God escort you out now and take you to the place assigned for you. It is not with me. Not any longer.

Spirit of fear, exit my life now. Exit my life forever. The angels of God escort you out now and take you to the place assigned for you. It is not with me. Not any longer.

Spirits of incest, rape, abuse, domestic violence, domestic terrorism, exit my life now. Exit my life forever. The angels of God escort you out now and take you to the place assigned for you. It is not with me. Not any longer.

Wounds infected by evil, you are now healed, in the Name of Jesus.

Holy Ghost, fill me. Fill me with Your Spirit, Your Power, Your Grace, Your Peace, Your comfort, to overflowing, that I pour it out to others, in the Name of Jesus.

Lord, do a new thing in me today. Break me out of old patterns and flesh reactions. Lord, give me the Mind of Christ and the ability to respond to life's stresses in a Godly way, in an unpredictable way, so the devil can not guess what I will do next, in the Name of Jesus.

A free Bird leaps. On the back of the wind. And floats downstream till the current ends and dips his wing and the orange sunrays and dares to claim the sky.

The free bird thinks of another breeze. And the trade winds soft through the sighing trees and the fat worms waiting on a dawn bright lawn and he names for sky for his own.

Maya Angelou, *I Know Why the Caged Bird Sings*

Any attacks because of these prayers, I command those attacks to backfire, in the Name of Jesus.

I seal these declarations across every realm, age, dimension, and timeline, past, present, and future, to infinity, in the matchless Name of Jesus Christ.

Amen.

Dear Reader

Thank you so much for acquiring and reading this book. I pray it has blessed you tremendously.

Dr. Marlene Miles

Other books by this author

AK: Adventures of the Agape Kid

AMONG SOME THIEVES

As My Soul Prospers

Behave

Blindsided: Has the Old Man Bewitched You?

Churchzilla (The Wanna-Be Bride of Christ)

The Coco-So-So Correct Show

Demons Hate Questions

Do Not Orphan Your Seed

Do Not Work for Money

Don't Refuse Me Lord

EVIL TOUCH

The FAT Demons

got Money?

Let Me Have a Dollar's Worth

Living for the NOW of God

Lord, Help My Debt

Lose My Location

Made Perfect In Love

The Man Safari *(Really, I'm Just Looking)*

Marriage Ed., *Rules of Engagement & Marriage*

The Motherboard: *Key to Soul Prosperity*

Name Your Seed

Plantation Souls

The Poor Attitudes of Money

Power Money: Nine Times the Tithe

Seasons of Grief

Seasons of War

SOULS in Captivity

Soul Prosperity: Your Health & Your Wealth

The *spirit* of Poverty

The Throne of Grace, *Courtroom Prayers*

Warfare Prayer Against Poverty

When the Devourer is Rebuked

The Wilderness Romance 3-book series, *The Social Wilderness, The Sexual Wilderness & The Spiritual Wilderness.*

Notes:

Notes:

www.ingramcontent.com/pod-product-compliance
Lightning Source LLC
Chambersburg PA
CBHW061336040426
42444CB00011B/2951